COMMUNICATING
THE GOSPEL
GOD'S WAY

COMMUNICATING THE GOSPEL GOD'S WAY

CHARLES H. KRAFT

William Carey Library

1705 N. SIERRA BONITA AVE. • PASADENA, CALIFORNIA 91104

Third Printing, 1983

Published by
WILLIAM CAREY LIBRARY
P.O. Box 40129
Pasadena, California 91104
Telephone (213) 798-0819

Library of Congress Cataloging Card Number 80-53945
ISBN 0-87808-742-7

Originally published as Volume 12, Number 1
of the *Ashland Theological Bulletin*, Spring 1979.

Reproduced by permission.

PRINTED IN THE UNITED STATES OF AMERICA

CONTENTS

INTRODUCTION TO THE ORIGINAL EDITION

"Communicating the Gospel God's Way" is the focus of the issue of the **Ashland Theological Bulletin** for 1979. The creative material by Charles H. Kraft appearing here was presented as the Workman Lectures at Ashland Theological Seminary, November 20 through 22, 1978. Dr. Kraft, who combines specializations in anthropology and linguistics, applies his rich resources to process and impact in communicating. These chapters, perceptive with insight and profound with understanding, offer both guidance and challenge to people for whom effective communication is important.

Charles H. Kraft, a 1960 graduate, was named "Alumnus of the Year" by Ashland Theological Seminary in 1978. He received the B.A. degree from Wheaton College with major work in anthropology and did graduate work in linguistics at the University of Oklahoma before completing his B.D. at Ashland in 1960. The writer received the Ph. D. degree from Hartford Seminary Foundation in 1963 with an emphasis on anthropological linguistics.

Dr. Kraft is currently professor of anthropology at Fuller Theological Seminary, School of World Mission in Pasadena, California. He served as missionary with the Brethren Church in northern Nigeria from 1957 to 1960. He has returned to Africa on many occasions as a field linguistic and ethnological researcher on Chadic languages and received a Fulbright-Hays Center Faculty Award for the study of Chadic languages.

The writer is one of the principal authors for studies in the Hausa language. He has published numerous articles and spoken widely concerning practical anthropology, African languages, Christianity and culture, cross-cultural communication, missionaries and indigeneity, and general Bible translation.

Dr. Kraft, an ordained minister in the Brethren Church, his wife Marguerite, and their four children reside in South Pasadena.

Owen H. Alderfer, Editor

CHAPTER I

GOD'S MODEL FOR COMMUNICATION

A S ONE who specializes in communication and Bible translation I am increasingly fascinated by the communicational dimensions of the Word of God. I am, of course convinced that God knew what He was doing communicationally. I am, however, surprised that it has taken us so long to look at the Bible from this point of view. For generations, we who seek to communicate God's Word have looked to the Bible for our **message**. I am afraid, though, that we have seldom looked to the Bible for our **method**. I have become personally convinced that the inspiration of the Bible extends both to message and to method. My aim in this chapter, therefore, is to elucidate a scriptural method for getting God's message across that I dare to call "God's Model for Communication."

Though I will be talking about what I believe to be a method of approach that we see from cover to cover in the Bible, it might be helpful, by way of introduction, for me to point to a couple of scripture verses which, if translated from a communicational point of view, lend support to the point I am trying to make. Look, for example, at Mark 16:15. It is, I think, allowable to translate this verse: "Go into all the world to communicate the Good News to all peoples." The word "preach" that is ordinarily used in English translations of this verse is only one way of communicating. Indeed it is a form of communication that Jesus used very seldom. I will deal more with this point in Chapter 4. Suffice it to say here that we are commanded by God not simply to monologue his Word but to communicate it as effectively as possible. A second illustrative verse is John 1:14. In this verse the Greek word **logos**, ordinarily translated "word" is employed. I believe it would not be doing the verse an injustice to suggest the following translation: "the (meaning God's) message became a human being to live among us." I will be alluding to other passages of Scripture as I go along but I wanted to point briefly to these verses at the beginning of my presentation to alert us to the fact that, in the first place, God is concerned about communication and that, in the second place, God's ultimate method of communication is via incarnation.

Now the problem I want to raise is: How can we follow God's example in our efforts to communicate his Good News? God has, of course, communicated very effectively. He has, furthermore, involved us in the contemporary phase of His communicatonal efforts. How then can we learn to involve ourselves in His work in His way? We do not believe that God simply overrules our humanity to make us into communicational robots. We believe that He leads us as we participate with Him in such activities. We believe also that we need to do our best to learn how He wants us to conduct ourselves so that we may be of greater service to Him. We may, therefore, analyze God's communicational activities as portrayed for us in the Scriptures in order to learn how He goes about His work so that we will know better how to go about our work for Him.

Another way of putting this is to use a term that is increasingly coming into prominence in Bible translation theory. This term is "dynamic equivalence." Our aim communicationally is to perform in a way this is dynamically equivalent to God's communicational activity as portrayed in the Scripture. A dynamic equivalence Bible translation is a translation that has the kind of communicational impact on today's hearers that the original Scriptures had on the original hearers. Such translations as Phillips, Good News for Modern Man, and Living Bible have often had such an impact in contemporary English. If you can imagine yourself communicating the messages that God gives you as effectively as these translations communicate the Scriptural message, you will have a glimpse at least of what I am talking about as the goal of Christian communication.

Preliminary Observations Concerning God and His Communicative Activity

The first thing I would like to deal with in this regard is to suggest six preliminary observations concerning God's communication. I believe that these observations apply to all of Scripture. I also believe that if we seek to be Scriptural in our communicative activity, we will seek to imitate God in each of these areas.

In the first place, I would like to suggest that God seeks to **communicate**, not simply to impress people, You have all had the experience of sitting in church and hearing a soloist or an organist or even a preacher show off in front of you. You may

4

have expected that they were going to communicate some message to you but, as they got into their performances, you began to realize that they were seeking only to **impress** you. They were of course communicating something, but that communication had more to do with their own ability than with anything they were talking, singing, or playing about. They seemed to be more interested in impressing people than in communicating with people. One basic principle of communication that is involved in such a situation is that when a vehicle of communication calls attention to itself, the message is lost. If, therefore, in a situation such as the preaching, singing, or organ playing situation, we become more aware of the performer's ability to perform than of the message he is seeking to get across, then the situation becomes a performance rather than a communication.

What I'm suggesting is that God **communicates** not simply performs. Throughout the Bible He uses language that does not call attention to itself. He uses people who do not call attention to themselves. In fact, when, as in the case of Saul these people begin to call attention to themselves, they become unfit for God's service. Likewise with respect to Bible translation, where the beauty of the language calls such attention to itself that it obscures the message. The Scriptures in the original languages are fairly unimpressive from a literary point of view. Jesus, when He walked the earth was also, apparently, fairly unimpressive personally. But His message had great impact.

Secondly, God wants to be **understood** not simply admired. God, of course, is impressive. He is, of course, to be admired. But there is a sense in which if we focus on merely admiring God, His ultimate purpose in interacting with human beings is thwarted. Some would seem to give the impression that God has an enormous ego that demands that people sit around admiring Him at all times. This seems to be the way in which many define worship. Without denying the value for us of contemplating God's greatness and of worshipping Him, however, I would like to suggest that His greater desire is that we understand and obey Him. Though not infrequently what God says and does is difficult for us to understand, God's ultimate purpose

is not "to mystify the truth" but to reveal it, not to hide verities behind historical accounts, but to face man with the truth in any and all literary forms which they can understand (Nida 1960:223).

As pointed out above it is in order to be understood that God used human language. It is to be understood that He took

5

on human shape, both in the incarnation and in the Old Testament theophanies (e.g., Genesis 18, Daniel 3:25). It is to be understood that God used dreams to reach those who believed in dreams and parables to reach those who had become accustomed to being taught through parables. On occasion God communicates through a spectacle (e.g. I Kings 19:11 & 12). But the spectacle is not an end in itself, it is merely the means to the end of effective communication that God employs in order to be understood. Likewise with miracles. John points to this fact by constantly labeling Jesus' miracles "signs." They are intended to point beyond themselves, to communicate something, so that God's message can be understood. This is why Jesus ran from those who were only interested in the spectacle for its own sake, but spent countless hours with those who got at least part of the message. He sought to be understood, and responded to those who responded to what he was seeking to communicate.

In the third place, let us note that God seeks **response** from his hearers not simply passive listening. This is a corollary to God's desire to communicate and to be understood. Communication implies response. When God commands people he expects them to respond. God's promises to people typically require a response on their part. Proper response in turn, elicits further interaction between God and human beings. Indeed, God's interactions with human beings are characteristically in the form of dialog, rather than monolog. The Bible, from beginning to end, represents God as seeking conversation with people. And such conversation demands responsiveness on the part of human beings. We are not simply to sit like bumps on logs listening to God without responding to him. To quote Nida again

> The entire concept of the covenant of God with man is predicated upon two way communication, even though it is God who proposes and man who accepts. Of course, in Jesus Christ the "dialogue" of God with man is evident in all of its fullness, but the divine human conversation is eternal, for the end of man is for fellowship and communion with God himself, and for this the communication of "dialogue" is an indispensible and focal element (1960:225).

A fourth preliminary point is the suggestion that God has revealed in the scripture not only **what** to communicate, but **how** to communicate it. I will not seek to elaborate this point at this time. I simply want to make the point explicit and to suggest that if what I have said above and what I will say below is true, this point is established.

My fifth preliminary point is to suggest that God is **receptor oriented.** In the communication process we have three basic

6

elements: the communicator, the message and the receptor. The communicator, as he engages in the process of communication, may have his attention focused on any of the three elements. That is, he may focus so intently on himself and what he is doing in the situation that he is virtually unaware of exactly what he is saying or of who he is attempting to say it to. Or he may be so focused in on what he is saying that he virtually forgets both himself and his receptors. Or, in the third place, he may so focus on his receptors, their concerns and the value of what he is saying to them, that his concern for himself and those aspects of the message that are not relevant to his hearers is diminished. This latter is what I mean by the term receptor oriented. Each of these approaches involves all three elements. They differ only with respect to which of the elements is in primary focus.

The communicator whose primary focus is himself tends to show off. One who seeks to impress people with his own abilities in order that they will admire him tends to fall into this trap. It may matter little to him whether people understand what he says or if they benefit from it. His concern is to be admired. The communicator who is message centered, on the other hand, gives great attention to the way the message is phrased. His concern is for precise terminology and correct wording on the one hand, and for and elegantly constructed, well balanced presentation of the message on the other. Again, the concern is less for whether the receptors understand the message than for the presumed accuracy of the formulation of that message. His tendency will be to resort to technically precise language, whether or not such language is intelligible to his listeners, and to homiletically perfect organization, whether or not his listeners are most attracted to that kind of a message. A receptor oriented communicator, on the other hand, is careful to bend every effort to meet his receptors where they are. He will choose topics that relate directly to the felt needs of the receptors, he will choose methods of presentation that are appealing to them, he will use language that is maximally intelligible to them.

What I am suggesting is that God's communication shows that he is squarely in the latter position. He is primarily oriented toward getting his message into the minds and hearts of his receptors. That is, the methods chosen, the language employed, the topics dealt with, the places and times where he encounters human beings and all other factors indicate that God is receptor oriented. He does not, of course, always say what people like to hear. That is not required of one who is receptor oriented. The point is that whatever he says, whether it is pleasant or unpleasant, is presented in ways and via techniques that have maximum relevance to the receptors. They do not have to go somewhere else, learn someone else's language, or become something other than they already are as a precondition to hearing his message. The message itself, of course, may require that they go somewhere else or become something else, but they are not required to make these adjustments **before** they can understand what God is saying to them. I will elaborate further on this point below.

In the sixth place, I'd like to suggest that God's basic method of communication is incarnational. Though the ultimate incarnation of God's communication was in Jesus Christ, God's method of using human beings to reach other human beings is also an incarnational method. In a real sense, everyone who is transformed by the power of God and genuinely lives his witness to Christ is an incarnation of God's message to human beings. It is not, I think, without significance that the early Christians at Antioch were called "little Christs," "Christians." God's witnesses are called by Paul "letters that have come from Christ," (II Corinthians 3:3). This is incarnational communication. And even the Bible, since it consists almost entirely of case studies of such incarnations of God's communications, may be seen as an incarnational document.

God's Approach: A Model for Us to Imitate

I would now like to turn to ten characteristics of God's communication. In doing this I have in mind three primary aims: to describe at least certain of the characteristics of God's communicational activity, to point out how well these correspond with the insights of modern communication theory, and to suggest that each characteristic is something that we ought to imitate in our attempts to communicate on God's behalf. I make no apology for the fact that these characteristics frequently take us into territory already covered in the above list of preliminary observations. Those broader observations and these narrower characteristics are, after all, simply alternative ways of viewing the same territory.

1. The first characteristic to note is that God communicates with **impact**. Impact is that which makes an impression, that gets people up doing things in response to what has been communicated to them. To get an idea of the kind of impact that God's communication had on people, we might simply ask ourselves what it would take to get us to do some of the things that

the people of Scripture did. What would it take to stimulate Abraham to leave home, country, family and all that was familiar to him? What was it that impelled Moses to stand up against Pharoah? What transformed the prophets, or the disciples, or Paul? The Holy Spirit was involved to be sure. But they were human beings who responded to communicational stimuli just like we do. So our questions concern not whether or not the Holy Spirit was involved, but what kind of response they as human beings had to the communicational techniques that God employed with them. The point is that they received God's communication with the kind of impact that impelled them to things that the world might regard as strange.

Now, we have learned to think of communication as largely a matter of the tranfer of information from communicator to receptor. We set up schools, we write books and articles, we preach sermons, in order to buy and sell information. When we go to school, read books or go to church, we are rather like the Athenians about whom it is recorded that they were primarily concerned with "talking or hearing about the latest novelty" (Acts 17:21). If we hear a lecture or a sermon or read a book that disappoints us we very often express our criticism by saying, "I didn't learn anything new." But the primary aim of God's communication, and hopefully of ours, is not simply to inform. It is to **stimulate** people to action. And when, via sermonizing, God's message is reduced to mere information about God rather than the passing on of stimulus from God, I wonder if we have not thwarted His purpose to some extent? The God who, through communicational channels, has had such an impact on our lives that we are in the process of transformation, desires that we communicate for him with a similar kind of impact. The characteristics by means of which He brings about that impact are delineated in the next nine points.

2. To create communicational impact, God takes the initiative. God does not simply sit there unconcerned. When Adam and Eve got into difficulty, God took the initiative and went to where they were to initiate the communication that would enable them to at least know how to get out of their situation. When he decided to destroy mankind, God initiated communication with Noah. Likewise with Abraham, Moses, and with person after person throughout Scripture. In Christ, God took the initiative that resulted both in His most significant communication and in salvation for humanity. We learn, therefore, that as communicators from God, the initiative lies with us.

9

3. When God seeks to communicate He moves into the receptor's frame of reference. I use the term "frame of reference" to designate the combination of things such as culture, language, space, time, etc., that make up the matrix within which the receptor operates. Each person operates within several frames of reference simultaneously. At one level, every person is in his own frame of reference defined by those psychological, physiological and life history characteristics that make him uniquely different from every other individual in the world. At another level, however, each person shares with many other people a language, a culture, a geographical area, a time frame, and many other similar characteristics. If, therefore, a communicator is to be understood by his hearers, he will have to start by employing such definers of broader frames of reference as the same language, similar thought patterns, and the like and proceed to demonstrate a concern for the characteristics that define narrower frames of reference such as the personal interests and needs of the receptor.

Not infrequently, especially when the communicator has some power over the receptors, the communicator will designate his own frame of reference as that within which the communication must take place. He may, for example, use a technical type of language that he understands well but that loses his receptors. Professors and preachers often do just this when they use the jargon and thought patterns of the academic discipline that they have studied when talking to people who are not normally a part of that frame of reference. Those who train for the ministry by going to seminary often get into the language and thought patterns of the seminary to such an extent that it may never occur to them that what they have learned needs translation into the language and thought patterns of their receptors if it is to have the desired impact on them. Many preachers, in fact, spend a large part of their ministries preaching to their homiletics professors. They have not learned that they need to use a different style to reach the people in their pews, so they simply continue to speak within the frame of reference that they learned to use in seminary.

God, however, is not like that. He uses the language and thought patterns of those to whom He speaks. He could have constructed a heavenly language and required that we all learn that language in order to hear what he has to say to us. He has the power to do that. But He uses that power to **adapt** to us, to enter our frame of reference, rather than to **extract** us from our frame of reference into something that He has constructed. He has, apparently, no holy language, no holy culture, no sacred set of cultural and linguistic patterns that He endorses to the exclusion of all other patterns. He moves into the cultural and linguistic water in which we are immersed in order to make contact with us.

4. God's communication has great impact, furthermore, because it is personal. Unlike modern Americans, God refuses to mechanize communication. If He had asked our advice concerning how to win the world, we might well have suggested that He use microphones and loud speakers. Or, perhaps, we would have suggested that He write a book, or at least go on a lecture tour where He would be able to monolog with thousands of people at a time. But the God who could have done it any way He wanted turned away from such mass impersonal techniques to use human beings to reach each other human beings and, ultimately, to become a human being himself. And as a human being He spent time with a small number of other human beings, running away from crowds in order to maximize the person to person nature of his interaction with that handful of disciples. We have much to learn from God's method at this point.

5. God's communication, then, is interactional. Note in your own experience the difference of impact between an impersonal, mass communication type of situation and a person to person interactional type of situation. I'm really impressed with how little Jesus monologed. And our misunderstanding of his communication that leads us to recommend monolog preaching as if this were God's method disturbs me greatly. In the name of Jesus Christ who seldom monologued we recommend monolog preaching as the appropriate method of communication! It seems to me utterly inexcusable for our Bible translators to reduce the nearly thirty Greek words used in the New Testament for communication to two words in English: preach and proclaim. But this is what has been done in most of our English translations. If one term is to be used in English, that term should be "communicate", not preach or proclaim, both of which signify monolog presentation. I am afraid we have not imitated Jesus in church communication nearly so much as we have imitated the Greek love for oratory. Jesus seldom, if ever, monologued. He interacted. I will say more about this in chapter 4.

6. A further characteristic of effective communication that God employs is that He goes beyond the predictable and the stereotype in his communicative efforts. It seems that in all

interaction, including communication, people either have or develop well defined expectations concerning other people. These expectations are defined in terms of such things as role relationships, age differences, linguistic and cultural factors and the like. On the basis of our previous experience with people in such categories, then, we develop stereotypes in terms of which we predict what is likely to happen when we interact with people who fit into a given category. When our prediction comes true— that is, when the person acts according to our expectations— the communicational impact of whatever that person says or does is very low. If, on the other hand, that person acts or speaks in a way that is unexpected in terms of the stereotype, the communicational impact is much greater. The principle may be stated as follows: if within a given frame of reference the information communicated is predictable, the impact of the communication will be low. If, however, within that frame of reference the information communicated is unpredictable, the impact of the communication will be high.

That's why, in Phillipians 2:5-8, we see Jesus going through a two-step process. He could easily have become man, and, as man, simply announced that he was God. But reading between the lines of the passage, we see that as a human being he refused to demand the respect that he had a right to demand. He refused to use his title. Nobody was going to call him Reverend or Doctor. They did eventually call him Rabbi, but they learned to call him Rabbi on the basis of what he **earned**, rather than on the basis of what he demanded. And I think this is a critical difference. Jesus established his credibility, earned his respect, by what he did **within** the receptors' frame of reference. He called himself man (i.e., Son of man) until they recognized him as God. And even when the disciples recognized that he was God, he forbad them to use that title for him. I believe he did not want others to use a title that he had not earned in interaction with them anymore than he wanted the disciples to. People have, of course, well defined stereotypes of God. If, for example, he had remained in his predictable glory or even, as a man, associated predictably with the powerful, the elite, the religiously safe people, the impact of what he sought to communicate would have been comparatively small. But he went beyond the predictable stereotypes at point after point and thereby increased enormously the impact of his communication. He went beyond the predictable to become a human being, and then even as a human being went beyond the predictable to become a commoner, and then as a commoner chose to associate with tax collectors and prostitutes, to go to such places as a raucous wedding feast and even to submit to a criminal's death.

As human beings, we too are boxed into stereotypes by those who interact with us. We are stereotyped according to our age group, whatever titles we possess, the kinds of people we associate with, the kinds of places we go to, etc. If we have a title such as Reverend or Doctor, if we fit into a category such as student or teacher, if we are male or if we are female, people will relate to us according to their expectations of the category by means of which they label us. And it is unlikely that they will pay much attention to the messages that we seek to communicate as long as those messages are according to their expectations from a person in our category. If, for example, we are known to them as Christians," and we say the kinds of things that they expect Christians to say, they may discount most or all of what we say. The impact of the communication will, however, be quite different if they find that we care for them more than they expect Christians to care for them or if we relate to them in a more genuine manner than they expect.

7.   God's communication, then, goes beyond generalities to become very specific to real life. And such specificity increases the impact of these messages. Many general messages are, of course, quite true. The general message, "God is love," for example, is unquestionably true. But his love put in the form of such a general statement has very little communicational impact. His love put in the form of a specific Christian individual, ministering to the specific needs of someone in need, however, has great impact. Even in language, the difference in impact between the statement, "God loves everyone," and, "God loves me," is great. Note in this regard the great difference in impact between the statement of a major point in a sermon and a well chosen illustration of that point that applies it to the real life situation of the hearers.

Jesus frequently used true to life stories that we call parables to specifically relate his teachings to the lives of his hearers. When someone asked him, "who is my neighbor?", he employed the parable of the Good Samaritan to make his teaching specific. When he sought to communicate truth concerning God as a loving father, he told the story we know as the parable of the Prodigal Son. He continually taught his disciples by dealing specifically with the life in which they were involved. He taught us all by ministering specifically to the needs of those around him. And the Bible that records these events is characterized by the specific life relatedness of a casebook. If God had communicated in our way, he might have written a theology textbook. Textbooks are noted for the large number of general and technical statements that they make concerning their subject matter. A casebook, however, is characterized by the kind of specificity to real life that the Bible is full of. The Biblical accounts concern specific people in specific times and places with specific needs that are dealt with by means of specific inter- actions with God. God, in his communication, goes beyond the general to the specific. So should we.

8. God's communication invites personal discovery: The most impactful kind of learning is that that comes to us via discovery. In our western educational procedures, however, we seem to go largely against this principle. As a teacher, I'm supposed to predigest the material that I want to communicate to you and to simply dish it out for you in a form that requires little effort on your part. In school, we get predigested lectures followed by testing techniques designed to force you to get that material first into our notebooks, then from our notes into our heads. Our churches have been patterned after the lecture procedures of our classroom except that in church we give no exams. This means that church communication is largely ineffec- tive, since it imitates the predigestion method of the schools but does not include the testing technique that is counted on to at least partially compensate for the lack of discovery involved in this kind of communication.

Note, for example, the difference between your ability to remember those things that someone simply tells you and your ability to remember those things that you discover on your own. Jesus specialized not in predigesting information in order to present it to his hearers in bite size chunks, but in leading his hearers to discovery. This is why his answers were so often in form of questions. This is also why his hearers often found him to be difficult. When John the Baptist was in prison and sent his disciples to Jesus to ask if he was indeed the coming Messiah, Jesus did not give him a straight predigested answer. His answer was designed to lead John to a life transforming dis- covery. Likewise with Pilate when he asked Jesus if he was indeed the king of the Jews. Jesus seems to respect people too much to simply give them a predigested answer. I believe again, that the casebook format of the Bible is designed to lead us into impactful discovery learning that will transform our lives, rather than to simply increase our store of information concerning God.

14

9. A ninth characteristic of God's communicative activity is that He invites the receptor to identify with Himself. In incarnation God identifies with the receptor. By so doing, however, he makes it possible for the receptor to complete what might be thought of as the communicational circle. That is, when the communicator gets close enough to the receptor to identify with him, the receptor is able to identify, in turn, with the communicator. As receptors, we seem to be able to understand messages best when we perceive that the communicator knows where we are. If he is able to get into our frame of reference, to establish his own personal credibility with us, to get to specific messages that show us he knows where we are, then we will find our ability to relate to him and to his message greatly enhanced. When the communicator relates to us in such a way that we can say, "I'm just like that," the impact of his message on us is greatly increased. That is why it is so tragic when a preacher puts himself so high above his people that they can't identify with him. They may feel that he is not where they are and cannot understand them well enough to say anything helpful to them.

How, for example, do you respond when someone from the Kennedy family talks about poverty? We are likely to dismiss whatever they say on this subject on the assumption that they have never had to experience what they are talking about. On the other hand, how do we react when we hear a member of that same family talking about suffering and death? At this point we are likely to have quite a different attitude, since we know that they have experienced great tragedy in these areas and have, therefore, earned their right to speak to us concerning them. Before God came to earth in Jesus Christ, how credible was anything he had to say concerning human life? It is all quite different now, however. For we know that Jesus lived and learned and suffered and died as one of us. Because, therefore, he identified with us, we can relate to him. We could not identify with a book or a loud speaker, only with a human being. When, therefore, he says, live as I have lived, suffer as I have suffered, give as I have given, we can follow him.

10. The tenth characteristic of God's communication is that He communicates with such impact that people give themselves in commitment to His cause. This is an indication of the ultimate in impactful communication. It is not difficult to communicate simple information. It is only slightly more difficult to communicate in such a way that the receptor gets excited about what he

has heard. But to communicate in such a way that the receptor leaves what he is doing and commits himself to the cause of the communicator, this is the ultimate indication of communicational impact. Jesus said to the disciples, "commit yourselves to me." And they did, even to the extent that they defied the whole Roman empire. That's impact. That's the kind of communicator God is. And it is His example that we need to follow in our communicational efforts—not to get people to follow us but to mediate God's communication in such a way that they will follow Him.

CHAPTER II

THE CREDIBILITY OF THE MESSAGE
AND THE MESSENGER

What I want to do in this chapter is to elaborate on, apply and extend the principles that I pointed to in Chapter 1. The special focus of Chapter 1 was on the activity of God in communication. The focus of this chapter is to deal a bit more with the question of what we need to do to imitate God's model. I am excited at this point in my life about the fact that Jesus not only died for us but that He **lived** for us. Among the many aspects of His life that we ought to imitate is the communicational example that He set. I finished Chapter 1 with the contention that the ultimate impact of communication is to get the receptor to give himself for the cause of the communicator. God's communication, has of course, had that kind of impact on many of us in many areas of our lives. A large part of that cause, and therefore our commitment is communicational.

In I Corinthians 11:1, the Apostle Paul made what seems to be an arrogant statement. He said, "Imitate me as I imitate Christ." He put himself squarely on the line by making a statement like that. He did not say, as I have heard many contemporary preachers say, "Lord, don't let them see me, let them see Jesus only." Paul seems to know that if his hearers were going to see Jesus at all, it had to be **through** him, not apart from him. That is, as a communicator, one who stands before people with a message to get across to them one cannot avoid the fact that the process of winning people to someone else involves first the winning of people to one's self. The credibility of the communicator is, therefore, an integral part of the effectiveness of the communicational process. The messenger is not separable from his message.

Two experiences in my life have driven this point home to me in a remarkable way. The first was an experience I had with a very intelligent and otherwise perceptive seminary professor.

17

Unfortunately, he did not see the close connections between what he was and what he said. Or, at least, he tried to avoid responsibility for any contradiction between his life and his words. What he said was, "Don't do what I do, do what I say." Now, fortunately, his life was not that much different from what he recommended. So we had little difficulty accepting both what he said and what he did. But the philosophy that he articulated is communicationally bankrupt.

The other experience that drove the point I am trying to make home to me was a thought that came to me one day as I surveyed the territory in rural Nigeria where I served as the only missionary. The majority of the people there, unlike here in America, had never even heard the name of Jesus Christ. Thus, when we spoke of Him they had no background independent of the Christian witnesses in terms of which to judge what Jesus must be like. They could not read the Scriptures, they were not acquainted with the two thousand years of Christian history that are so familiar to us, they could only watch those of us who called ourselves Christian. As I pondered these things, the thought came to me that, from their point of view, I **am** Jesus Christ! And it blew my mind. I was forced to recognize that I stood squarely in the gap between them and God. To them Jesus looked like I looked, He acted like I acted, He loved like I loved, He spoke, He ate, He drank, He travelled, He lived as I did. If they were going to see the love of God that Jesus lived to express, they would have to see it through me. What a responsibility! And yet, such a responsibility is not unique to a missionary in a pioneer area of the world. It is the responsibility of each one of us who stands and attempts to communicate in Jesus' name.

With respect to incarnation God, of course, could go much farther than we can. He was able to incarnate Himself as a distinct human being in a particular language and culture of his choosing in such a way that he experienced the full biological and cultural process of birth, learning, living and death within that culture. We do not have such an option, given the fact that we have already been born into and taught by families that we did not have the luxury of choosing. Thus, when we seek to reach people who live in a frame of reference different from our own, we are always limited by at least two factors that Jesus did not experience when he participated in first century Hebrew culture. First of all, we have not learned the cultural basis of our receptors' frame of reference as children, and, secondly, we are always hindered in our attempts to understand our receptors by the fact that we have been trained into our own frame of reference. When speaking of human communication, therefore, we may better use the term "identification" rather than the term incarnation. We do this in recognition of the fact that the best we can do, even when we imitate God's incarnational approach, is to identify with our receptors. We can never fully enter their frame of reference as we might if we were born into it. Nevertheless, even though we must settle for something less than full incarnation, we may imitate God's communicational approach by doing our best to employ God'sprinciples. We assume, of course, that we are also doing our best to present God's message.

Employing God's Principles

1. The first principle is the major principle, that of being receptor oriented. This principle is so important that it is worth the risk of my repeating a bit to elaborate some more. As I write this, I have to deal with the question,"Where are you the readers? I don't know most of you, so I have to guess where you might be. I guess by attempting to analogize on the basis of my own experience plus my guesses as to who might be reading this. To some extent, since my experience has been quite similar to that of many of you, I will be able to guess where you are fairly accurately. At many points, however, I will probably misunderstand or misestimate where you are and, therefore, fail in one way or another to communicate what you need in a way that will enable you to make good use of it. There is however, great risk involved here—risk that I may either flee from by refusing to even attempt to communicate, or that I may take even though I know that I will be misunderstood. It is obvious which course I have chosen.

The point is that once we know enough to be receptor oriented, we must face certain important questions. We must ask, for example, where are the receptors? What are they interested in? What is it going to take to reach them? Then we need to ask ourselves questions concerning the risk factor. Should we deal with this topic? Are these receptors prepared to understand and make use of the material we present? Is their attitude towards us as a communicator such that they will accept messages from us on this topic. Then we must ask ourselves questions concerning the way in which we present the message. It is not enough that we as communicators speak truth. We must, therefore, pay careful attention to the way we present our messages, lest the way we make our presentations,

19

the language we employ, the attitudes we project, deter our hearers from understanding what we intend that they understand. Our concern for the importance of the message commited to us, therefore, requires that we, like God, be receptor oriented.

2. A Second point at which, I believe, we should be more careful to imitate God is at the point of taking the initiative. Just as God did not stand and wait for others to seek him out, neither should we stand and wait. We have to go figuratively as well as actually where people are. We often establish our churches and other Christian organizations in such a way that the only way people will know we exist is by coming to where we are. I might refer to this as a "yellow pages" approach to evangelization. It is easy to assume that people know we exist and that they are convinced of our relevance.

Now, I am not simply speaking of the way we place our church buildings. We cannot, of course, be proud of the "waiting game" that characterizes many of our churches. They seem to say, "The people know we are here, if they want us they will seek us out." My primary focus is, however, on something more subtle than the placement of church buildings. That is the fact that a person sitting right next to us in the same room may be psychologically even more distant from us than many people on the other side of the world from us. And if we are to imitate God, we need to take the initiative to reach out to that person also. Or, if you are a pastor, there may be a great psychological difference between you and many of the members of the congregation. You cannot simply assume that if they attend regularly, they are getting the messages that you think they are getting. You may not be getting close enough to them psychologically and communicationally for them to really benefit from what you are saying. They, on the other hand, may simply be attending church out of habit or because they feel that God will bless them more if they spend this time with his people. To reach them, you may have to take the initiative.

One aspect of taking the initiative is to not assume too much with regard to the credibility, the trust and confidence, that people have in us. If you are not well known to the people you seek to communicate to, of course, you must establish your credibility with them in order to be listened to at all. We often, however, ignore the sense in which, even when people know us well, we need to reestablish our credibility in each new communicational situation. Whatever the situation demands, then, with respect to developing a trust relationship between ourselves and our receptors, we need to take the initiative to establish our credibility. Another way of saying this is to suggest that we need to win the right to be heard in every communicational situation.

3. The initiative that we take, then, is to move toward the receptor, into his frame of reference. Just as God does, we need to employ the receptor's language, including his slang or jargon, key our message into his world of experience and interest, and over all refuse to give in to the temptation to force him into linguistic and conceptual territory that is familiar to us but not to him. The temptation to extract people from where they are into where we are in order that we may feel more comfortable in dealing with them is a strong temptation indeed. We found it at work on the mission field where people were encouraged to learn our language and our culture in order to adequately understand the message that we sought to communicate to them. As mentioned in Chapter 1, those who have been taught to understand and speak about God in theological terminology are very often tempted to require that their hearers learn to understand their language and thought patterns before they can properly understand the message of God.

Yet we often do not really know where our receptors are. One of the dangerous things that often happens to a person when he takes a pastorate or other Christian service position, is that he assumes that he knows where his people are. Preacher after preacher has had to find another pastorate, or even another occupation because that assumption turned out to be wrong. One problem is, of course, that we are trained in classrooms for occupations that are usually quite unlike anything that goes on in our classrooms. Some of our problems would be solved if we were trained to do things by **doing** those things rather than by simply **thinking** about doing those things. When we spend our time thinking about things we learn to think about things. When we do things we learn how to do things.

One pastor that I know did what I think is exactly the right thing. He took a pastorate in a small industrial town in New England soon after he graduated from college. He had, however, barely settled into that pastorate when he took a job in a factory. When the church leaders found out about this, they called him on the carpet. They knew they were not paying him the highest salary in the world, but they did expect him to be full time. His reply was something as follows "I am full time. All of the money I'm making in the factory is going right into the church. My problem is that I have spent all of my life to date in school. I just don't know where you people are. You are spending from 9:00 a.m. to 5:00 p.m. every day in the factory and until I have spent 9:00 to 5:00 day after day in the factory I'm not going to be able to speak effectively to you." This is the kind of identificational approach that I am recommending. His sermons from that time on were right where the people were. He was constantly talking about his interaction with the people on either side of him where he was working in the factory. He refused to assume that he knew where his hearers were simply because he'd been in school and studied a bit about them. He got out there and learned about his people by doing the things that they did in the kinds of contexts in which they spent their lives. He didn't work very long in the factory, he didn't have to. He only had to work long enough to get a feel for where his congregation was so that he could use this understanding to get into their frame of reference.

Anything not in the receptors' frame of reference is virtually unintelligible to him. We can bring in new information from outside into the frame of reference of the receptors, but everything depends on how we bring it in. People learn, apparently, by analogies. But these analogies must be familiar enough to them from within their experience to make the point that the communicator is trying to make. When the point is made, then, the receptors recombine the material that is already in their heads with the new material to arrive at new understandings. It is the job of the communicator to so present his new material within the receptor's frame of reference that the receptor can interact with it thoroughly enough to produce constructive new understandings within his head. I am not suggesting that we cannot present new material to our receptors. On the contrary, if we look at Jesus' example, we find that he frequently presented new material to his hearers. But he used familiar forms such as parables and analogies from the life experience of his receptors in order to maximize their ability to integrate the new information into their frame of reference.

4. But even though we may have effectively entered the receptor's frame of reference, there is still no assurance that we will communicate effectively unless we have gained the receptors' respect. As I have suggested in Chapter 1, there is a distancing that takes place when one allows himself to be called by a title. Titles designate stereotypes, assigned positions that people have in relationship to other people. But when you assign someone a position in some category other than your own category, you

isolate him from yourself. The title, the stereotype, enables you to predict not only the position of that person in relationship to yourself, but the behavior of that person. And if he conforms to that stereotype in his interaction with you, you say to yourself, "What should I expect?"

One very interesting indication of the kind of stereotype that preachers have in the minds of lay people is the way that the preacher in the Pogo comic strip is presented. All of the other characters in that comic strip are represented as speaking in ordinary type. But the preacher is presented as speaking in Old English type! This, I believe, is intended to show the kind of stereotype that people have of preachers. It is also a very clever way to represent in print the distance that is ordinarily understood to exist between preachers and common people.

What, then, is the answer to this problem? It is, I believe, to escape from the stereotype by refusing to be predictable in terms of that stereotype. Now, there are ways of not conforming to a stereotype that will ultimately hinder the communication. I am not suggesting that we employ means that would be inconsistent with the message that we seek to communicate. Nor am I suggesting that **anything** unpredictable that we might do will help the communication. I could, for example, use language in this presentation that would be both unpredictable and detrimental to the communication. There is, however, a kind of unpredictability that I would like to recommend that is both consistent with what Jesus did and a distinct asset to communication whenever we find ourselves boxed in by a stereotype.

5. What I would like to suggest is that we attempt to overcome the distancing created by a stereotype by becoming a **genuine human being** to our receptors. Think, for example, of certain stereotypes and then ask yourself the question what is the opposite of each of those stereotypes? You will discover, I think, that you, along with most other receptors, will tend to think of people as either preachers or human beings, either teachers or human beings, either young people or human beings, etc. This may be slightly overstated but only slightly if at all. I think there is an important truth in the observation that we tend to define people who are like us as human beings, while we define those on the other side of a stereotype boundary from us in terms of whatever the generalized characteristics of that stereotype seem to be in our minds.

I came across this fact in a dramatic way one time in Nigeria. I was discussing with one of my friends there some aspect of Euro-American culture when he remarked to me, "Fear God, fear the white man." This statement turned out to be one of their proverbs. And as I began to probe the meaning of the proverb, I became aware of the fact that we whites were not only distanced from them by their stereotype of us, but we were linked with God rather than with human beings in their minds. As I pondered this, it was not difficult for me to understand their point of view. From their point of view, only God and whites had the power to produce automobiles, bicycles, grain grinding machines, radios, airplanes, and the like. Furthermore, only God and whites could be so confident, self assured, free from fear and unpredictable. Human beings (that is, people like themselves) are not powerful, not wealthy, fairly predictable, not self assured, fearful, etc. So everything seemed to indicate that we fit into the God category rather than into the human being category. What I began to ask myself, then, was how am I going to become a human being to them in order that I might communicate to them on a person to person level?

What is the difference in your relationship with people between those who first get to know you as a human being and only later discover that you have earned a title, and those who first get to know you in terms of your title? Sometimes, if they first get to know you in terms of your title, you will then say and do things that cause them to remark, "Gee, you sure don't act like a _____." If you are a teacher, they may say, "You don't act like a teacher, you act like a human being." Of course, they usually do not articulate the last part of the sentence. They usually simply say: "You don't act like a teacher," or "You don't act like a preacher," or "you don't act like a Christian." But what they mean is that somehow you have broken out of the stereotype in terms of which they had been thinking of you and have become for them a human being. And actually, if becoming a human being to them is done in a proper way, it will enhance your ability to communicate to them.

I would like to suggest a five step process for escaping from a stereotype into the human being category of our receptors. The first step is to try to **understand** them. This is not always easy and it is not always enjoyable. Oftentimes we are called upon to attempt to communicate to people of whom we really don't approve. We may not even like them or approve of their lifestyles. But we must attempt to understand them in terms of their own frame of reference if we are to have any chance of becoming credible to them.

Then we must go beyond simply understanding them to **empathizing** with them. Empathy is the attempt to put ourselves in the place of those to whom we are trying to relate. It involves us in attempting to look at the world in the way that our receptors are looking at it. We may have to say to ourselves, "If I assumed the world to be what they assume it to be, how would I think and act?" If we properly understand and empathize, then, we should come to a fairly good understanding of what their definition of human beingness is. For it may be quite different from our definition.

And this puts us in a good position to take the third step, which is to **identify** with our receptors. Now, identification is a difficult concept. And many people have the wrong impression of it. They think identifying with others is becoming fake. And sometimes it can be. Many think of older people trying to speak young people's language, dress like young people and grow beards. But true identification is not being fake. It is not trying to **become** someone else. It is, rather, taking the trouble to become more than what one ever was before by genuinely entering into the life of other people. There are dimensions to most of us that we have never really probed. And identifying with another person or group, genuinely entering into his frame of reference, challenges us to probe another of these unprobed areas. One of the amazing things about human beings is that we can become bi-cultural. We can, by entering into the lives of other people, become just as real in that context as we are in our normal context. It takes more work, it takes a lot of learning, a lot of modifying. However, when we find our efforts paying off to the extent that people remark, "you are just like one of us," we begin to realize that it is very much worth it.

But in order to do this, we need to take the fourth step and to participate in the lives of the people we are trying to reach. Beyond simply identifying with them and their life is participating in it with them. This, of course, needs to be done with caution. But we see, I think, in Jesus' ministry a kind of fearlessness concerning what people might say about him when he went to even disreputable places and associated with even disreputable people. He "lost his testimony" for the sake of the people that he sought to win by participating with them in their lives.

The fifth stage, then, in attempting to become a human being in order to reach human beings, is what has been termed **"self exposure."** One could go all the way to the participation stage in this process and never really let others know what one is like beneath his skin. It is, unfortunately, possible to identify and participate with people without really giving one's self to those people. Thus, it is necessary to go beyond participation to self exposure. This is the practice of sharing one's inner most feelings with those with whom one participates. It is not the kind of questionable practice that some indulge in when they share intimate details of their inner life in their public presentations. It is, rather, the sharing of one's innermost feelings with those within the receptor group with whom one has earned intimacy. At this level, the confession of faults, doubts, and insecurities becomes a valid part of one's testimony rather than a disqualification of one's right to speak convincingly. I believe Jesus related to at least some (perhaps not all) of his disciples at this intimate level. Even our records show him at the self-exposure level when he cries over Jerusalem, when he casts out the money changers, and when in Gethsemane he begs God to accomplish his purposes in some other way than via death. Becoming a genuine, credible human being to our receptors takes us beyond understanding, empathy, identification and participation to this kind of self exposure.

One final word would seem to be in order before I turn to my next point. That is to point out that in order to reach people in a frame of reference other than our own in the way that I am recommending, we do not have to either convert to that frame of reference as our preferred way of life in the sense that we adopt our receptors' lifestyle, nor do we have to uncritically endorse that way of life. Certainly Jesus, by becoming a common person in first century Palestine, did not endorse every aspect of the lives of those with whom he participated. When, however, he spoke critically of their lives, he spoke as one who was committed to them as a participant in their lives rather than as an outsider who simply threw stones at them.

Perhaps this is why he got so upset with the Pharisee who, in the story recorded in John 8, sought to stone the woman taken in adultery. I believe part of what he was saying to them was that, unless they participated in real life the way she was forced to participate in it, and understood life from her perspective, and still could maintain their righteousness, they had no right to condemn her. I don't believe that Jesus condoned her activity, but neither did he condone the right of outsiders to condemn her according to laws that they, within their own context, were unable to obey.

When one lives in two worlds, all that is required is the acceptance of the validity of each way of life. We do not even condone much of what goes on within our own world, much less that that goes on within someone else's world. We must understand that their world, though it may differ considerably from ours, is no less valid as a way of life than is ours. And yet, we may still prefer our original frame of reference to that of those whom we seek to reach. There is nothing wrong with this. For there is no necessity for a bi-cultural person—one who has become more than what he was when he was simply monocultural—to convert to the second culture or sub-culture. He can, like Paul be a Jew with Jews and a Greek with Greeks (I Cor. 9:20) without losing his authenticity.

6. Now, as our sixth major point we turn to the credibility of the message that the communicator presents. Not only must the communicator himself/herself be perceived by the receptors as authentic and credible. His/her message must have the same kind of ring to it. And to do so the message must speak to the felt (or perceived) needs of those who hear it.

The whole matter of perception by the receptors is at this point (as at all other points) crucial. I once heard a theologian say, "There is nothing more relevant than the Christian message". He said this as if relevance is something that is attached to a given subject matter for ever and ever. Yet we have to ask the question: "If the Christian message is inherently relevant, why are so many people perceiving it to be irrelevant?" I believe the reason lies in the fact that relevance is **constructed** by the receptors in communicational situations. Relevance is as relevance is perceived. Again, as in all areas of communication, the final verdict is up to the receptor. If you take what I'm saying to be relevant it is because you have constructed it that way in this situation. You have received it as relevant. You have been able to connect it with something in your own experience, some need that you have come to feel. If you perceive what I'm saying to be irrelevant, then I've probably not been successful in trying to relate it to your felt needs. Perhaps I had assumed that you had needs in areas where you don't have needs. So you have been unable to construct this message as relevant to your particular situation.

The Gospel is like that too. It is not perceived as relevant by everyone, unfortunately. It would be very nice if it were. It would be very nice if we could just stand up here and do what some people recommend—simply present the Gospel as best we

27

can and leave the rest to God. In some sense, of course, we have to do that, for we are dependent on the Holy Spirit to bring people to respond to God. But there are disturbing instances where we think the Holy Spirit ought to make it relevant to people and and he doesn't seem to. Yet it seems that when I do my job better, the Holy Spirit usually does his job better. The variable in this whole situation, though, is not the Holy Spirit but me. So I need to do my best to present that message that has transformed my life in such a way that it is perceived as relevant to the people to whom I speak and before whom I live. And that means relating it to their felt needs.

Relevance and felt needs, though, are matters of the here and now. We are living now and so are our hearers. Yet the documents we work with (the Bible) are relating God's messages to other people in other times and places. And because of that fact it is easy to fall into the mistake of dealing with the Scriptures as if God's main intent were merely to provide interesting (or sometimes dull) history lessons or linguistic expositions. We who have trained for Christian ministry often have our minds so full of such a variety of interesting and helpful classroom-type details concerning the Scriptures that we insist on regularly transporting our hearers back into Biblical times and places rather than on understanding and interpreting Scriptural messages in relation to their felt needs.

I was taught in seminary that exegetical and expository preaching are better than topical preaching. The validity of this point lies in the fact that unless pulpit attention to current topics is solidly grounded in the Scriptures, it is unworthy of the Christian communicator. I think, however, that we need to add two important qualifications to any recommendation of exegetical or expository preaching: 1) if it is to be true to the relevance criterion here recommended (and, I believe, exhibited in Scripture), preaching must be topical enough to relate to the felt needs of these people at this time and in this place; and 2) that Jesus was always topical. To be Scriptural is, I believe, to deal Scripturally with topics perceived by our hearers to be relevant to their felt needs.

The concept of felt need must not, however, be understood as merely a superficial kind of thing. People do, of course, have needs of which they are aware. These are usually articulated in questions they ask at the surface level. And attention to these is often the only "gateway" by means of which a communicator will be allowed to get through to his receptors. Once he has made use of such a gateway, however, he finds increasingly deeper levels of need only some of which the receptors could have articulated early in the relationship. Some of these needs may have been there at the start but felt only at a subconscious level if at all. Some may have been developed during the process of the interaction. One thing that often happens in effective Christian communication is that trust and credibility of messenger and message is established at a fairly superficial (perhaps even trivial) level. Through interaction between the receptor, on the one hand, and Christians and the Scriptures, on the other, then, the receptor enters a process by means of which he discovers other needs that propel him to seek answers from Christian friends and the Scriptures. As he receives answers from these sources, however, he uncovers still other needs that need to be dealt with in the same way. And so on.

7. In keeping with our focus on relevance to felt needs, and in imitation of Jesus' model, we suggest next that the message needs to be specific to the real life of the receptors. As I have noted in chapter 1, this is one of the great things about the Scriptures. They present and deal with real life things. They consist largely of case studies of real people in real life situations. And even when Jesus taught via parables, these were true-to-life stories, many of which are so characteristic of real life that it is hard to believe that they didn't actually happen.

In Jesus' name, though, we often deal with our subject matter at such a general level that there is little or no perception of relevance on the part of our hearers. If we use good illustrations and/or get personal we are more effective because we have gotten specific. It is via the specificity of the illustration or the personal account, then, that whatever is communicated gets across, not via the general points in our outlines. And many an unaware preacher has effectively communicated something quite different via his illustrations that what he intended to get across!

I was at a large meeting of young people one time when I decided to test the degree to which the young people were paying attention to the speaker. So I worked out on a piece of paper what might be referred to as a makeshift "cough meter." There were nine thousand young people at that meeting and the weather was very cold, so nearly everyone was coughing. What I did, therefore, was to try to draw a line on my paper that indicated the level of the coughing. This line went up and down as the coughing level went up and down. What I observed was that while the speaker was dealing with the main points in his outline, the level of coughing was relatively high. When, however, he got specific, either in terms of an illustration or by describing his own personal experience, nine thousand young people stopped coughing! I remember clearly from that experience how attentive the young people became each time the speakers became personal. They seemed to be unconsciously evaluating the generalized presentation as something that could be ignored or, at least, as something to which they did not have to devote their whole attention. The specific illustrations and personal experiences, on the other hand, seemed to be evaluated as so important that they should devote their full attention to them. It might be useful to make this kind of observation in church as well. Observations of the level of coughing, fidgiting, clock watching and the like will probably lead you to the same conclusion that I have come to—that specific messages receive greater attention than general messages do.

8. As point number eight, then, I want to emphasize that, as with Jesus, the effective Christian communicator needs to lead the receptor to discovery. As I have mentioned, discovery learning is minimized by many of our American educational and church procedures. When, however, the communicator becomes a real human being, presenting his message in close specific relation to the receptors' felt needs, discovery is enhanced enormously. Case studies, illustrations, specific application to the real life of the hearers, raising questions for which the receptor must struggle for answers, and the like, are all helpful techniques for leading people to discovery.

The matter of the ease with which the receptors can move from material presented to application in their own life is again relevant here. We have been carefully taught that if we can present general principles, our hearers can easily make the applications. I don't blieve that is as true as we tend to assume. I think more often we find that communication is most effective when the communicator has presented something rather specific that we find we can relate to, because we discover that the specifics of what he is presenting and the specifics of our own experience are rather close to each other. I think, as I have said before, that it is easier to go from specific to specific than from general to specific. But even if the communication is from general principle to specific application, is much more impactful if the receptor discovers how the principle applies to his life than if the communicator points it out to him.

9. Much of what I have been saying here can be summarized in the principle, the messenger himself/herself is the major component of the total message. As much as we might like to avoid this kind of responsibility, as much as it frightens us to recognize the responsibility involved here, I believe we must accept this fact. For, as McLuhan has pointed out, the medium that transmits the message conveys a message of its own. Some people try to avoid their responsibility in this regard by attempting to separate widely between the message and their own behavior. The professor mentioned above who said, "Don't do what I do, do what I say" is a case in point. His approach was unrealistic at best, irresponsible at worst, though it must be said that a professor who only spends a few hours a week with his students might be better able to pull off such a philosophy than someone who has greater and more total involvement with those to whom he communicates. The major thing a professor (or a preacher) communicates is, however, what he does, not what he says. Indeed, the main thing we learn from professors and preachers is how to be professors and preachers, not as we think, the messages that they articulate verbally! For this reason I recommend in chapter four below what I believe to be a better total model for the kind of communication that we seek to get across as Christians.

We are a major part of the message that we seek to communicate. This is why it is so important if we are in a pastoral situation to spend as much time as possible with the people in our congregation. It is in visitation, rather than in preaching, that the majority of important communication goes on. Sermonizing is more like the display in a store window than like the merchandise on the counters. Store managers know that it is very important to have good display in the windows. But they also know that their business will not be successful if they spend all their time decorating the windows and none of their time making sure that they have good merchandise inside the store. A pastor, therefore, who spends most of his time preparing his window display (his sermons) and little of his time dealing with his people and the merchandise that he has to present to them on an individual level, will not be very effective in the Lord's business. Likewise a pastor who keeps a great distance between himself and his people. He may be able to perform well in front of his people but that performance becomes a part of his message. And people learn all kinds of strange things concerning God by observing such performances. The fact that God became a human being to reach human beings is not only

31

relevant as a technique for putting his messages across, it is an essential characteristic of the message itself. It is, furthermore, something that we must imitate if we are to accurately communicate God's message. Christianity is someone to follow, not simply information to assimilate. Our lives must, therefore, line up in support of both the person and the personalness of the Christ message. If our lives contradict that message, the information we seek to get across is worthless.

10. The tenth point, then, is that the communicator should aim to bring the receptors to identify with him and to commit themselves to his cause. As we have seen, this is the ultimate impact of effective communication. Jesus did this and we follow him because of it. Now we are to do it and to bring others to follow us as we follow Christ (I Corinthians 11:1). Jesus was God's incarnation for his day. Now, in a very real sense we stand in his shoes as God's message incarnated for this day. If we present our message in the way that I have been recommending, our receptors will see both us and our message as vitally related to themselves and their needs. Some of them, then, will choose to identify with us, not only as human beings but as communicators of the message that they find transforming their lives. They respond with receptor identification and commitment to our cause. This is an indication that the Holy Spirit has been doing his work, but it is also an indication that we have communicated effectively. And this is our ultimate aim in imitation of Christ to whom we have responded in identification and commitment to his cause.

CHAPTER III

WHAT IS THE RECEPTOR UP TO?

We have focused in chapters one and two on God's model and the application of that model on the part of the communicator. Now we turn to a focus on the receptors. We may take as the text Romans 10:14-17 the intent of which can, I believe, be adequately summarized as "faith results from understanding and responding to the message effectively communicated." We have suggested that a communicator needs to be receptor oriented. We have also indicated that receptors construct the meanings that result from communicational situations and then respond to those meanings that they construct.

1. My first point in this regard is that the receptors are not passive. One mistake that older theorists of communication made was that receptors are rather like sponges, simply soaking up the messages that are sent their way. If, however, we try to analyze our own activity as we converse with someone or sit in the audience listening to a lecture or sermon, we begin to realize that we are anything but passive. Indeed, as we interact with someone in conversation, we may find that often we are not listening as we should to what the other person is saying. We are too busy constructing what we are going to say in response. Or as we sit listening to a lecture we may find that our thoughts are miles away or that we are in our head arguing with the speaker rather than simply listening to him.

The fact seems to be that in any communicational situation there are many things going on at the same time. At any given time when we are listening to a speaker, we may be more concerned with how he is saying something than with **what** he is saying. Or we may be more focused in on the way he looks than we are on what he is saying. Or we may be more concerned with the person next to us or with someone else in the audience than we are either with the message or the messenger. Those of us who have listened to countless sermons and lectures may, in fact, have gotten into the habit of picking the message apart he speaks. I have spent my time in any number of sermons and lectures doing just that. In fact, there is probably not a sermon or a lecture that I cannot find something wrong with, especially if I don't want to be listening to it in the first place.

Or, we may be listening intently to the communication and interacting positively with everything that is said. But even then, we are anything but passive. We are actively interacting with the communication, whether we are accepting it, rejecting it, or avoiding it.

2. My second point is that one of the most important kinds of activity that receptors engage in is the activity of constructing the meanings that result from the communicational interaction. Older theories of communication saw communicators simply putting together and passing along words and phrases that contain their meanings. The receptor might or might not understand what is being said, because he might or might not understand the meanings of the words and phrases employed. But, according to these older theories, all the receptor needs to do to arrive at the intended meanings is to find out the proper meanings of the words and phrases. For, these theories contend, the meanings lie in the message itself.

Recent communication theory, however, has abandoned that rather mechanical view of communication in favor of a more personalistic view. Contemporary understandings contend that a major difference between messages and meanings lies in the fact that messages can be transmitted in linguistic form while meanings exist only in the hearts and minds of people. Contemporary communiologists see communicators with meanings in their minds that they would like to transmit to receptors. Communicators take these meanings and formulate them, usually in linguistic form, into messages which they then transmit to receptors. Receptors then, listen to the messages and construct within their minds sets of meanings that may or may not correspond with the meanings intended by the communicator.

Meanings, therefore, do not pass from me to you, only messages. The meanings exist only within me or within you. I have certain meanings in my mind that I would like to get across. I try to formulate these in terms of messages, whether verbal, written or in some other form. In the case of this transaction I am formulating my meanings via writing. You, then, read my messages and construct within your mind the meaning that you consider to be appropriate to the messages that I am sending. If you are positively disposed toward me and my messages, it is likely that you will construct meanings that are at least favorable toward what I am trying to say. You might still misunderstand what I am saying, but you are likely to give me the benefit of the doubt. If, on the other hand, you are negative toward me and/or my messages, you are likely to attach unfavorable meanings to the messages that I send whether or not you understand them. The messages, then, serve as **stimulators** rather than as containers. Receptors, in response to the stimulus of messages construct meanings that may or may not correspond to what the communicator intended.

The significance of this particular insight is extremely important to all of us who seek to communicate effectively. It means that if I am going to get across to you I am automatically accountable both for the way I construct the message and for the impact of that construction upon you. This means that I am accountable to understand as much as I possibly can concerning how you are likely to receive my messages. And this relates strongly to your previous experience with messages of this kind. If I know you, I am able to predict with a fair degree of accuracy how you will respond. If, however, I do not know you, my ability to predict your response may be severely hampered. Suppose, for example, I speak or write like someone with whom you have had a bad experience. The meanings that you construct from my messages are going to be affected by that fact. And the ultimate verdict concerning what results from the communicational situation will be affected by circumstances largely beyond my control.

I can present you with information in the best way I know how. But if I don't really know you, the way I present that information can be based only on my best guess as to where you might be and how this type of presentation might affect you. I will try to use words, phrases, and the like that you will both understand and toward which you will be positively disposed in order that you will give my messages at least the benefit of the doubt. But I may not guess right. Or, I might naively employ terminology that I happen to like that raises red flags in your mind.

Suppose, for example, I like the word "liberal." Suppose the word has for me a positive connotation and I start talking about the glories of being a liberal. I suspect that the audience to which I am now writing would be strongly inclined to be negative both toward me and toward my message if I tried to use that word in a positive sense. If, on the other hand, I identify myself as a "conservative," particularly with regard to theological issues, my guess is that the audience to which I am writing would take a positive attitude toward me and my message. In either case, the communication that I seek to get across is affected to a greater extent by the meanings that you the audience attach to the words and phrases that I employ than it is by the meanings that I attach to those symbols. And if I don't realize what is going on, it would be very easy for me to stimulate in your minds meanings that are quite distant from the meanings that I intend.

The importance of this particular fact in communicational situations was once driven home to me in a way that I cannot forget. I was asked by a very conservative church to give a series of Wednesday evening lectures on the subject of Bible Translation. As near as I could tell the first lecture was received quite well. But when I appeared the next week for the second lecture, I was informed by the leader of the group that some of the people were complaining about me because I did not use the phrase "the blood of Christ" in my lecture the previous week. I suggested to the leader that the omission of that phrase had more to do with the subject matter about which I was talking than with any position that I might have against the sacrificial work of Christ. His reply was that he well understood my point of view but that if I could insert that phrase somewhere in my discussion this week, it would help considerably in the communicational situation. Now, what was going on here was the fact that those who were listening to my message were not sure whether they should construct meanings that they considered orthodox or meanings that they considered liberal from my message. They did not know me and were not sure about my credibility. So I decided to take their request seriously and provided them with a fairly detailed testimony concerning to my Christian experience. After that they all relaxed and we had a good series of interactions. They were looking for something that would stimulate meanings of trust in their minds. Their message to me, then, was couched in the words "blood of Christ." I guessed correctly what they really meant by this symbol and provided them with a personal testimony—an alternate symbol that enabled them to attach the meaning "orthodoxy" to my messages. And we had a good relationship after that.

The point is that one of the important activities of receptors is the constructing of the meanings that they attach to the messages to which they are exposed. These meanings are consructed by attaching particular meanings—both denotative and connotative—to the symbols via which the message is presented. Those symbols, the words, phrases, sentences, etc., in which the messages are couched, are not, therefore, like box cars that carry the same meaning wherever they go. They are more like darts, thrown to prick people at certain points in order to stimulate in them certain kinds of responses.

People communicating in the same language do, of course, attach largely similar meanings to the same words, phrases, etc. This is because as parts of a single linguistic community, they have all been taught to attach similar meanings to the same symbols. But even within the same community there is a greater or lesser range of variation in the meanings that various members of the community attach to the words they use. There is very seldom, if ever, a complete correspondence between the meanings in the head of the communicator and the meanings in the heads of the receptors. The approximations may, however, be fairly close and the communication quite adequate, in spite of the lack of a total correspondence between the communicator's meanings and the receptors' meanings. In any event, it is crucial for the communicator to recognize that the receptor is active in the process of meaning construction and to do everything he can do to assure that the receptors' activity in this respect will be closer to rather than farther from what he communicator intends.

3.   Another activity that the receptor engages in constantly is that of evaluating the message. It is apparently a basic of our humanity that we not only participate in experiences but we evaluate them. In a communication experience then, we evaluate each compound of that experience, including the communicator (whether someone else or ourselves), the message, and the receptors. If we are the receptors in a given situation, we constantly evaluate the message in relation to ourselves, including our past experiences, our present experiences and whatever we are projecting for ourselves in the future.

One aspect of our evaluation relates to the total situation. We evaluate such aspects as place, time, other persons involved, manner of dress of the participants, the temperature, the arrangement of persons, furniture and other accoutrements, and all other features of the communicational situation. From this evaluation we construct an overall impression of the situation. This overall impression then, has much to do with how we interpret what goes on in that situation. You know how differently you react in a given situation if you evaluate it positively from the way you might act in a similar situation that you evaluate negatively or neutrally. You are also aware of the fact that in some situations your impression is strongly positive or strongly negative, while in other situations your impression is only mildly positive or mildly negative. The point is that we evaluate all situations in which we participate and that this is one primary form of activity in which we engage as receptors.

In addition to evaluating the total situation, however, we constantly evaluate each part of the situation. Indeed we may find ourselves positively disposed to a total situation but negatively disposed towards certain of the people in that situation, certain of the messages communicated in that situation, or even our own participation in the situation. In any event, receptors certainly are not passive in communicational situations—they are constantly evaluating them.

4. Another kind of activity in which receptors are engaged is the matter of selectivity. Receptors are selective with respect to at least four areas. The first of these is with respect to what kinds of things one will be exposed to. Those of you who are reading this have chosen to be exposed to it. There are probably many others who glanced at this material and decided not to expose themselves to it. In our everyday lives we are constantly selecting those things that we want to be exposed to and those things that we do not want to be exposed to. There are, of course, many reasons why we choose to expose ourselves to certain things but not to others. Not infrequently the choice to expose ourselves to some things relates more to our desire to please someone else than it does to our interest in that to which we expose ourselves. But whatever the reason the fact is that receptors are active with respect to choosing what they will expose themselves to communicationally.

Not infrequently, though, we find ourselves in a position where we are exposed to communications that we would rather not be exposed too. Sometimes our spouses, or children or friends drag us to some communicational event against our wills. Or, we may have to attend something because it is required by our job, our role, or some social involvement in which we find ourselves. At times like these we have another kind of activity that we can employ as receptors. That is selectivity of attention. We may not be able to avoid being exposed to given messages, but we may find it possible to only pay attention to certain parts of those messages. We may sort of blip in and blip out while the communication is taken place. Or we may allow ourselves to get easily distracted by something else that is going on. Either way, we pay attention only to certain aspects of the communication. Sometimes we are so inattentive that we mentally go off into a distant land or even fall asleep. At such times selective attention comes quite close to selective exposure.

A third area in which receptors exercise selectivity is in the area of perception. It is not always possible to avoid exposure or even to avoid paying some attention to the message. But we tend to perceive messages in such a way that they confirm already held positions, whether or not the communicator intended them that way. This is usually done unconsciously and relates to our overall evaluation of the situation and the various components of it. One person with a given attitude toward a communicational situation may perceive and even distort the message in one way while another person in the same situation but with a different evaluation of it will perceive or distort the message in quite another direction. Whether or not we understand the message also plays an important part. The perception that we take away from a communicational situation may be distorted as much by partial understanding or even misunderstanding as it is by our evaluation or because of our understanding, we are consciously or unconsciously selective in our perception of the messages that we hear.

Our intention when we go into a communicational situation likewise has much to do with what we perceive from that situation. If for example, we go into a situation seeking comfort or distraction or entertainment, we are likely to come away from that situation having gotten what we came for but missing whatever else the communicator might have intended. Or, if we go into a situation with high expectations concerning what we will obtain but find nothing to meet those expectations, we may well go away from that situation totally disappointed having perceived only in terms of the negating of our expectations while having missed many valuable things that we could have obtained had we been less selective in our perception.

The fourth area in which receptors are selective is in the area of recall. On occasion, we may be exposed to a message, pay attention to it, and even perceive it correctly, but when we remember back to that occasion at a later date, we may choose to remember only a certain selection of the things that we actually heard. This choice is usually made in terms of those things that fit in most easily with the things that we already believed and felt. That is, if we have a positive attitude towards ourself and the communicator said things that fit in with that positive attitude (no matter what else he said), we may well remember only those things. If, on the other hand, we have a negative attitude towards ourselves, and the communicator said things that fit in with that predisposition, it is likely that we will recall those things, even if the communicator said many things that were contrary to this predisposition. I will develop this point further in the next section. Suffice it to say that in at least these four ways receptors engage in the activity of selection in communicational events.

5. Receiving communication is a risky business. Receptors are, therefore, continually active in dealing with the risk. As we read this, or as we sit listening to a communicator speak, we may have little conscious awareness of the risk factor. And yet, whenever we expose ourselves to communication we are risking the possibility that we might have to change some aspect of our lives. We ordinarily seek at all costs to maintain our present equilibrium, to protect ourselves from assimilating anything that will upset our psychological balance. To do this we often build walls around ourselves in such a way that we can shed much of what we hear that would cause us to change our lifestyle. By means of the selectivity of which we have been talking, we refuse to take seriously much of what we hear. We refuse to process information, to be concerned about it, to see the implications of such information for our lives. Or, even if we do see the implications, we often refuse to work such insights into our lives. One thing we often do, of course, is to apply what we hear to someone else's life in order to avoid having to take it seriously ourselves.

These strategies that we use are often referred to as "coping strategies." A coping strategy is a way of dealing with the threats that come to our equilibrium from such sources as ambiguity, unanswered questions, and incomplete assimilation of new information. In school, of course, we are bombarded with so much information that we learn well how to cope with information overload by shedding most of it. We may learn enough of it well enough to pass whatever examinations we have to face, but we develop the habit of refusing to process most of it. We also learn, however, to defend ourselves against much of the information that we do process. The so called "critical thinking," that we are taught to employ is often no more than defensive thinking, designed more to protoect us from considering new ideas than to evaluate those ideas in terms of their potential value to us. We learn to say, "yes but . . .," to nearly all new ideas in order to minimize the risk to our psychological equilibrium that a serious consideration of new ideas would entail.

Note what frequently happens in this regard when we listen to someone speak. If they are on the other side of an experience gap from us, we may protect ourselves from risk by saying to ourselves as they speak, "Yes, but he doesn't understand where I am." If the communicator has a status such as preacher, teacher, or someone else we regard as having "made it," we may say to ourselves, "Yes, but he doesn't have to face what I have to face." If the speaker seems to be dealing with a complex issue at a fairly superficial level, we may avoid the risk of taking him seriously by saying to ourselves, "Yes, but he has terribly over-simplified things." If the communicator increases the risk by keeping good eye contact with his receptors, the latter may use various strategies to keep from having to look the communicator in the eye. In these and similar ways, receptors are very active in attempting to reduce the risk involved in communication situations. Even agreeing with people without seriously considering what they say may be a coping strategy engaged in by some to avoid or reduce the risk factor in communication.

6.   Another kind of activity that receptors are involved in is the production and transmission of what is called "feedback." As the communicator speaks, his receptors are active in sending messages back to him. These messages, or feedback, serve various purposes in the communicational interaction. Often the receptor wants to encourage the communicator. He may, therefore, smile, nod, make some short comment or in some other way show his approval of what the communicator is saying. On the other hand, receptors often want to provide the communicator with negative feedback. In English speaking situations we often shake our heads, frown, or make short negative comments to provide negative feedback. Quite often the receptor produces and transmits feedback at a subconscious level. As receptors we may fidget, cough, show rapt attention, either seek or avoid eye contact, or in other ways quite unconsciously send feedback to communicators. Sometimes, indeed, as receptors we carry on a rather full internal conversation with the communicator of which he is rather completely unaware. Whatever of this surfaces in such a way that the communicator can read it becomes feedback.

The constructing, sending and receiving of feedback in communicational situations is a rather intricate business. Often receptors construct and send a good bit of feedback that is not picked up by the communicator. If, for example, the communicator has been brought up in such a way that he has not learned to read the particular feedback that the receptors construct and send, there can be a considerable amount of miscommunication. Often, in our society, fellows and girls are trained into quite different feedback systems. It is not uncommon for a girl to send large amounts of feedback that are never picked up by the fellows with whom she associates. Often such feedback is constructed in rather elaborate "hints" that are not responded to by fellows. Those who construct and send feedback, therefore, must also be receptor oriented, in the sense that they must be careful to send the kind of feedback that is intelligible to their receptors, if they are to be correctly understood.

7. The final type of receptor activity with which I would like to deal is that of coming to a verdict concerning the communication. The receptor needs to do something about the communication. He has to decide whether to act on the communication or to ignore it. If the communication simply involves information, as with a news broadcast, he needs to decide whether to try to remember it or to simply forget it. If the communicator is appealing for a change in his behavior, he needs to decide whether to respond positively, negatively or neutrally to that appeal. Whatever the decision the receptor comes to concerning the communication, some kind of a verdict, some kind of a judgment is involved.

Suppose the verdict is to ignore some sort of persuasive communication. The receptor may decide to judge that the communication is directed to someone else, or that the communication should be regarded as a performance rather than as an appeal, or that he is already performing what is being recommended. Any of these, or other decisions with respect to communication, qualify as verdicts made by the receptor.

One of the verdicts that we often make in classroom situations is what to do with the notes we take on the lectures that we hear. We recognize that we cannot possibly remember all of the things presented to us by the lectures we listen to, so we choose to record some of the more important things on paper. Then we have to decide what we do with the notes. We are often helped by our professors to use those notes at least one more time to review for examinations. But after that, we must decide whether to store them in our files or not, and if we store them, when and how often to consult them.

If the communication has been of a persuasive nature, such as much Christian communication is supposed to be, the receptor has to decide whether or not to identify with the communicator and if so whether or not to commit himself to the cause of the communicator. As I have suggested in previous chapters, the ultimate impact of Christian communication is indicated when receptors decide to identify with the communicator and to commit themselves to his cause. This is the kind of verdict we are after as Christian communicators, whether we are speaking evangelistically or attempting to bring about great growth toward maturity on the part of the receptor.

42

CHAPTER IV

THE POWER OF LIFE INVOLVEMENT

The topic that I want to deal with in this chapter is something that will, on the one hand, serve as an illustration of a number of things that I've said above and on the other hand, as a probe into some new areas that are important to us as Christian communicators. I'd like to suggest as texts Matthew 4:19 and John 10:11-15. In Matthew 4:19 (and Mark 2:14; Luke 5:27, etc.), Jesus says, "Come along with me." The word "follow" in many Semitic and related languages implies "come along with" or even, "commit yourself to." It is not the kind of thing that one would say to a dog to get it to follow. It is a matter of commitment. I would then like to pick out of the passage in John 10, particularly verses 11-15, the implication that not only would the Good Shepherd die for the sheep, but that the Good Shepherd would also **live** for the sheep. I think that is strongly implied in the whole section.

A few years ago I began to ask myself about the communicational **means** that we use to bring about the ends that we desire. I asked things like, what are we trying to bring about through church services? I concluded that we are trying to bring about behavioral change. That is, we want people who are so solidly influenced by our message that their behavior is radically affected. Whether it is the behavior of people who have not yet committed themselves to Christ, or the behavior of those who have already started on the road, our aim is to try to deepen and broaden their commitment.

I further asked, what kind of communication methodology is appropriate for trying to bring about that type of behavioral change? And, if monolog is not the best method for appealing for behavioral change, what is it good for? In grappling with these questions I began to develop a typolgy of approaches to communication in which I try to summarize several elements of three approaches to communication. The first approach is the monolog approach. The second is the dialog or discussion approach. The third approach is what I label "life involvement." The following chart outlines the items I discuss below.

43

A TYPOLOGY OF APPROACHES TO COMMUNICATION

CHARACTERISTIC	APPROACH I (Monolog)	APPROACH II (Dialog)	APPROACH III (Life Involvement)
1. METHOD OF PRESENTATION	Monolog/Lecture	Dialog/Discussion	Life Involvement
2. APPROPRIATE TYPE OF MESSAGE	General Messages	Specific to Thinking Behavior	Specific to Total Behavior
3. APPROPRIATE AUDIENCE	Large Groups	Small Groups	Individuals or Very Small Groups
4. TIME REQUIRED FOR GIVEN AMOUNT OF INFORMATION	Small Amount	Medium Amount	Large Amount
5. FORMALITY OF SITUATION	Formal Dominant	Informal Prominent	Informal Dominant
6. CHARACTER OF COMMUNICATOR	Reputation Important	Personality Characteristics Important	Total Behavior Important
7. FOCUS OF PARTICIPANTS	Source Dominant (Message)	Message Prominent (Source-Receptor)	Receptor Prominent (Source-Message)

44

8. ACTIVITY OF RECEPTOR	Passive—Merely Listens	Considerable Mental Activity	Total Life Involvement
9. CONSCIOUSNESS OF MAIN MESSAGE	High (Both Source and Receptor)	Medium	Low (Perhaps Contradictory Verbal Message)
10. REINFORCEMENT AND RETENTION	Low	Medium	High
11. FEEDBACK AND ADJUSTMENT	Little Opportunity	Considerable Opportunity	Maximum Opportunity
12. DISCOVERY BY RECEPTOR	Little—Message Predigested	Considerable Discovery	Maximum Opportunity for Discovery
13. TYPE OF IDENTIFICATION	Source Identifies Primarily with Message	Reciprocal Identification with Each Other's Ideas	Reciprocal Source—Receptor Identification on Personal Level Over All of Life
14. IMPACT ON RECEPTOR	Low—Unless Felt Need Met	Potential High on Thinking	Maximum on Total Behavior
15. APPROPRIATE AIM OF APPROACH	Increase Knowledge	Influence Thinking	Influence Total Behavior

1. In the above typology the first characteristic to deal with is the method of presentation. We all know what monolog is. We experience this form of communication as the almost exclusive method used in sermons and lectures. Dialog or discussion, on the other hand, is more frequently employed in situations like Sunday School classes, Bible studies or other smaller group experiences. Many situations that look like dialog situations are, of course, merely opportunities for a leader to monolog. The leader may or may not allow serious discussion type interaction on the part of the others in the group. Such a situation would fall under the monolog column rather than under the dialog/discussion column.

The third method of presentation, here termed "life involvement," may not be as readily understandable as the first two, however. What I am thinking of here is a long term association between communicator and receptors in a variety of life situations, many of which might be quite informal and not highly dependent upon verbalization as the only means of communication. Discipleship and apprenticeship are examples of this kind of communicational method. In discipleship the teacher spends long periods of time with his disciples in a wide variety of life activity. Jesus and his disciples were together twenty-four hours a day for three years. In apprenticeship, an apprentice spends long periods of time with his teacher in a variety of work related activities.

Another illustration of life involvement communication is the family. As we grow up within our family we are life involved with our parents, with our siblings and not infrequently with a variety of other relatives, neighbors and friends. We may or may not like everything about the way we have learned to live from such life involvement, but the fact is that we have learned our lessons well. We have become very much like those with whom we have associated.

The question that I am asking concerning the method of presentation is, if we seek to bring about genuine solid, deep, behavioral change in the people to whom we try to communicate the Christian message, can it be effectively done via monolog? Jesus seldom, if ever, monologued. Is it possible He rejected this method of communication because He considered it inadequate for the purposes that He had in mind? Did he, on the other hand, choose life involvement as his method because he knew that this was the only adequate method for accomplishing his purpose? If so, could it be that we have been misled into depending heavily upon a method that the Church has learned more from Greek orators than from Jesus?

2. In the second place I would like to ask, what type of message is appropriate to each method of presentation? Though we may note that solid behavior change seldom results from monolog presentations, we also observe that much of value can be accomplished. Perhaps, then, the problem is not so much that one method is appropriate in all contexts while the other method is never appropriate, as it is that we learn to use each method in the context in which each is most appropriate. Indeed, suppose you have a general message about which there is some urgency such as, "Your house is on fire." It would, I think, be poor advice to suggest that such a message be presented via dialog or life involvement! Monolog is the proper methd for that kind of message. Likewise for a general message such as "Two and two are four." Unless you are in the initial stages of teaching someone basic addition it is unlikely that a communicator would take the time involved to dialog that message either. News broadcasts and other presentations of a purely informational nature are also effectively presented via monolog.

If, however, your aim is to affect your receptors at a deeper level than simply the information level, it is likely that monolog will not adequately serve your purpose, unless, of course, what you present via monolog connects strongly with one or more of the felt needs of your receptors. In that case, as I have pointed out, nearly any method will work because the receptor is so anxious for the material presented that he will accept it and appropriate it no matter what form it comes in. But for situations that go beyond the mere presentation of information to receptors who do not have a strong felt need for the message, some other approach is likely to be necessary if our aim is to bring about some change in the receptor.

For this purpose we can recommend dialog as an appropriate way to seek to bring about change in the receptors' thinking behavior. Dialog, of course, is a type of life involvement. It is, however, very often quite limited with respect to time, place and the extent of the areas within the lives of the participants over which involvement takes place. But for wrestling with differences in the thinking of the participants, dialog might be quite adequate. If, however, the aim of the message is to affect the receptors' total behavior, the depth and breadth of the change brought about is quite dependent upon the ability of the receptor first to realize what is being recommended and then to imitate it. And this involves what psychologists call "modeling." Though it is possible for receptors to imagine Christian models or, on occasion, to be able to recall previous experiences with such models, the most effective modeling comes from live involvement between the communicator and the receptors. In the preceding chapters I have already dealt with many of the aspects of a life involvement approach to communicating Christianity. This is, I believe, merely another way of talking about an incarnational methodology.

3. These methods differ with respect to the appropriate size of audience. With very large audiences, monolog is perhaps the only possibility. It usually does not work very well to attempt to dialog with a large group. And life involvement with very many is completely out. To some extent, of course, we are life involved even when we monolog with a large group. But this is in a very minimal way and the few things receptors learn from such life involvement with lecturers center largely around getting used to the lecturer's style, mannerisms, facial and vocal expression and the like. The general rule, then, is large groups for monolog, smaller groups for dialog, and still smaller groups for life involvement.

Could Jesus have operated in a life involvement way with more than twelve disciples? Probably not. In fact, even with dialog the numbers involved cannot be very large. Notice what happens to Sunday School classes when the attendance grows beyond, say, twenty-five to thirty. If the class continues to use a dialog format, the number on the roll may continue to rise but the attendance will usually level off at about twenty-five to thirty at most. This seems to be the optimum number for dialog in our society. If the number attending the class gets to be much larger than this, the teacher will ordinarily change to a monolog method. Almost invariable, when there are large Sunday School classes, they are conducted on a monolog basis. We don't seem to be able to handle discussion with more than a small number of peole. And with apprenticeship or discipleship, the number that can be handled is even smaller.

4. Our fourth consideration is to ask the question, given a certain amount of material to be gotten across, how much time would each method require? In a monolog format, it does not take very much time to present a fairly large amount of information. Note, however, that is it merely information, rather than something that is likely to have a greater impact on the receptor, that is being presented. I believe that our attachment

to preaching and lecturing has affected Christianity enormously at this point. By using a monolog format so exclusively, we have come to treat Christian communication as primarily the passing of large amounts of information from communicators to receptors. We have come to focus primarily on information that we should know in order to be Christians rather than on learning a life that is to be lived. I believe this is a serious distortion of the Christian message. The amount of crucial information involved in Christianity is, I believe, quite small. The amount of Christian behavior demanded in response to that information is, however, quite large. We have, however, given ourselves to a methodology that emphasizes the lesser of the two ingredients.

Be that as it may, it is clear that a monolog method is better at presenting large amounts of information, while a life involvement method is better at applying smaller amounts of information to larger areas of behavior. Dialog, then, fits somewhere in between. The amount of information that can be presented in a given amount of time via dialog is not very great, especially when campared with monolog. But it is certainly greater than is possible with life involvement.

5. The fifth consideration is a matter of the formality of the situation. Though not all monolog situations are extremely formal, they tend to be more formal than either dialog or life involvement. Life involvement situations, on the other hand, tend to be considerably less formal than either of the other two. Dialog/discussion situations fall somewhere in between. I will not go into further detail concerning the formality of communicational situations, except to suggest that formality affects communicational impact by defining the social distance between communicator and receptors. If that social distance is perceived by the receptors to be great, that fact will affect the kind and nature of the messages at every point. Likewise, if the social distance is perceived to be small and the relationship between the communicator and receptors perceived to be intimate.

6. In the sixth place, I would like to raise the matter of the perceived character of the communicator. In general, the greater the social distance entailed in the communicational situation, the more important the reputation of the communicator is to that situation. When deciding whether or not to attend a lecture, we are greatly concerned with whether that person has the credentials, the reputation to enable him to deal with the topic in a helpful way. Advertisements for lectures, therefore, focus strongly on the credentials of the lecturer. In

49

such formalized situations, there is little opportunity for the receptors to assess for themselves the overall credibility of the communicator, except as he deals with that subject in that situation. It is highly desirable, therefore, that the trust level of the audience already be high before the communicator makes his presentation.

In dialog, and especially in life involvement situations, there is much more opportunity for receptors to make their own assessment of the communicator's ability. Though it is still desireable for the communicator to be perceived as credible and trustworthy going into the communicational situation, there is much more opportunity for receptors to modify their original opinions of the communicator in more intimate communicational situations. Often, for example, receptors go away from a lecture situation with essentially the same attitude toward the speaker with which they started. In more intimate situations, however, receptors are often much more impressed with the communicator, both with respect to his subject matter and with respect to himself/herself as a person. On the other hand, students exposed to teachers over small periods of time in classroom situations are often quite impressed with their teachers as long as their exposure is limited to those formalized situations. If, however, a student gets to know his teacher in other areas of life, he may discover some things about that teacher that cause him to revise his opinion downward, even to the point is discounting the validity of the things communicated by the teacher in the classroom. This of course, quite often works the other way as well, especially with respect to teachers who might not be particularly effective in formalized classroom situations who happen to be outstanding persons overall.

7. In monolog situations, furthermore, the focus of the participants is squarely on the source, with the message also in focus but to a lesser extent. Receptors are much less in focus. The chairs are set up in such a way that everyone faces the communicator. All eyes are on the front of the room. It is expected that people will sit quietly and take all of their cues from the speaker rather than from anyone or anything else in the room

In a dialog situation, on the other hand, there is often an attempt to arrange the furniture in a circle, down playing the importance of the leader to some extent. The discussion, then, will focus on grappling with the subject by means of a lively interchange between leader and receptors. Thus the message

50

comes into greater prominence as do the receptors, while the prominence of the communicator diminishes a bit in comparison to his prominence in a monolog situation. In life involvement, then, it is the needs of the receptors that come strongly into focus. The activity of the communicator and the nature of the messages are bent to the meeting of the particular needs of the receptors. In Jesus' case, though he was in complete control at all times, the choice of the subjects with which he dealt and the manner in terms of which he dealt with them shows a strong primary focus on meeting the needs of his followers.

8. As I have pointed out in chapter three, receptors are not inactive. In a monolog situation, however, receptors tend to be considerably less active than in discussion and life involvement situations. When we listen to lectures or sermons, we basically just sit there. Things are going on in our minds and, at least in classroom situations, we may be taking notes. But our activity is often the more mechanical activity of simply ingesting the material as it is presented, rather than the more demanding activity of considering the material in relation to our total life experience with a view toward incorporating it into our lives. It is that kind of activity, however, that discussion and life involvement communication forces us into. This is why many people dislike more intimate communicational situations where they will be forced to answer questions or in other ways to indicate the kind of deep level interaction with the material that is going on within their minds and hearts. They consider such a process too threatening to be comfortable.

9. Given the fact that in every communicational situation there is a multiplicity of messages being sent, we ask, in the ninth place, what the level of consciousness of the main message might be in each of these approaches to communication. In a monolog situation, of course, the intention of the communicator is that the main message will be strongly in focus. And, unless he/she acts in such a way as to distract from the main message, or unless something else distracting happens while he is presenting that message it is likely that that message will be in primary focus. If, however, the communicator breaks some rules by, say, standing too close to certain of the members of his audience, or by belching during the course of his presentation or by wandering around the room during the presentation, it will be these strange things rather than the main message that will be remembered.

In discussion situations, and particularly in life involvement situations, however, the messages communicated regularly go far beyond the main message. Messages concerning the openness of the communicator, his kindness, his patience, his ability to deal with problems that he may not have anticipated, his ability to integrate the things about which he speaks into his own life, and similar messages are often strongly communicated along with the main message. Indeed, for many of the receptors the way in which the communication is dealt with becomes a more important message than the primary topic itself. Not infrequently, then, these additional messages, technically known as "paramessages," cancel out much or all of the main message. This leads, then, to responses such as, "Your life speaks so loudly, I can't hear what you're saying."

In life involvement, it is often the tone of voice or the timing of the message that indicates to the receptor that the most important message is not the one being verbalized. Often, for example, a sharp or angry response has more to do with the communicator's discomfort than with the receptor's needs. Such a situation is indicated, for example, by the reported response of a bright child when her mother told her to go to bed. Her response was, "Mommy, how come when **you** get tired, **I** have to go to bed?" The mother might well have felt that she was communicating only the "go to bed" message. But the perceptive child picked up a paramessage that was probably more accurate as an explanation of the situation than the message that the mother wanted to be in focus. In life involvement, then, what is communicated goes far beyond what might be regarded as the main message.

10. Learning is highly dependent upon what is termed "reinforcement." That is, messages that we hear once and never again tend to be crowded out by messages that we hear over and over again in a variety of ways and applied to a variety of contexts. Our tenth point is, therefore, a consideration of the opportunity for reinforcement and the consequent likelihood that the receptor will retain the messages presented via each of these approaches. The monolog approach, of course, due to such factors as the generality of the messages, the large amounts of information involved, and the small amount of interpersonal contact between communicator and receptors, provides little opportunity for the messages to be reinforced and is, therefore, likely to result in low retention on the part of the receptor. Dialog provides considerably more opportunity for reinforcement

and, therefore, much more likelihood of retention. Life involvement, then, is especially adapted to provide large amounts of reinforcement and to result in correspondingly large amounts of retention. Note, for example, what happens to reinforcement and retention when, after a lecture, the audience engages in a lively discussion with the communicator concerning certain of his points. The communicator, then, has opportunity to illustrate, to explain, and to apply certain of his points much more fully. Receptors will typically respond to such a situation by indicating that they now have a much higher level of understanding than they obtained from the lecture. If, then, a certain few of those who listened to the lecture and participated in the discussion are able to spend long periods of informal time with the lecturer, perhaps even living with him for awhile, his ability to reinforce his message and their ability to retain are increased enormously. Pastors should know that the ability of their hearers to retain messages presented in their sermons is substantially increased by visitation and other informal techniques designed to increase a life involvement relationship between themselves and their hearers.

11. Feedback and the opportunity of the communicator to adjust his message on the basis of it is of great importance in the process of communication. There is, of course, little opportunity for feedback in a monolog situation, more opportunity in a discussion situation and a maximum opportunity in a life involvement situation. An audience who perceives that the communicator has chosen the wrong message in a monolog situation may, therefore, have little opportunity to let him know in hopes that he might adjust. In a life involvement situation, on the other hand, there is maximum opportunity for the hearers to get such a message back to the communicator and a high likelihood that if the communicator does not make the proper adjustments, his audience will leave him. Indeed, the formal nature of most monolog situations is often the only thing that keeps the audience from completely dissipating.

12. All of this has great implications for the amount of discovery learning that the receptors may engage in. As I have suggested above, discovery learning is the most impactful kind and the kind that Jesus employed. Monolog, of course, emphasizes the predigestion of the message at the expense of discovery on the part of the receptors. Life involvement, on the other hand, specializes in leading the receptors to discovery. Discussion is somewhere between these two extremes. In dialog and life

involvement situations especially, and to a lesser extent in response to certain sermons and lectures, we find people saying, 'Wow, I haven't thought of that before." Such comments are an indication of discovery learning. We find the disciples making comments like that throughout their experience with Jesus.

13. The primary type of identificational process is the thirteenth characteristic in our typology. In a monolog approach it seems as though the source attempts to identify primarily with his/her message and perhaps to a lesser extent with the receptors. In dialog, on the other hand, the identification seems to be more reciprocal between communicator and receptor, though often primarily at the idea level. Life involvement, then, involves reciprocal identification between source and receptor at a highly personal level and over the whole of their lives. In terms of what I have said above, concerning the importance of the receptors may be to identify with the communicator, it is easy to see the superiority of dialog and life involvement as communicational techniques. I will suggest below certain modifications that can be made in monolog presentations to overcome the more disastrous possibilities of that approach in this regard.

14. All of this leads to an assessment of the communicational impact on receptors of communication employing each of these approaches. The impact via monolog is likely to be quite low unless one or both of the following situations exist: (a) The felt needs of the receptors for the material being presented are high, or (b) the communicator makes the kind of adjustments in his presentation that I speak about below. Dialog communication, on the other hand, has high potential for impact at least on people's thinking behavior. Life involvement, then, has the potential for maximum impact on the total behavior of the receptors.

In employing sermons, lectures, or the kind of written medium that I am employing here, we count on at least certain members of our audiences coming to the situation with a need for what we are presenting. Our ability to communicate effectively to them, then, is highly dependent upon our ability to guess where their felt needs lie. Sometimes, of course, we guess very well. On other occasions, however, our guesses may be quite wide of the mark. Certain communicators, furthermore, seem to be either unconcerned or unable to guess well at any time. Others, happily, seem to be able to regularly transcend the probability factors in their ability to communicate effectively via monolog. Some of the reasons for this may lie in the factors that I discuss below.

15. I ask, therefore, as point fifteen, what the appropriate expectation should be in our use of these three approaches. It seems that if our aim is simply to increase the knowledge of the receptors, that monolog is the appropriate method. If, however, we seek to solidly influence the thinking of our receptors, we should use a dialog/discussion method. Influencing total behavior, however, demands much more total life involvement than either of the other methods affords. As I have mentioned before, monolog can be effectively used much like a display in a store window, to alert people to the good things that await them once they get beyond that display. Monolog is also good at bringing people to make decisions that they have been considering for a long time. Monolog can, furthermore, be usefully employed to support people in decisions that they have already made. This is probably the major function that sermonizing serves in our churches and over the mass media. Studies of the use of sermons via radio and television point out, however, that very few people who do not already agree with the communicator either listen to the presentation or have their opinions affected by them. And those who do have their opinions changed via mass media are almost always those whose felt needs predispose them to be positive toward the kind of change there advocated. Even then, however, the durability of the opinion change is highly dependent upon the continued reinforcement of a group of like-minded people. This is one of the primary functions of the church within Christianity. Monolog does, however, enable us to present large amounts of information in a relatively efficient way. The church's over-dependence on monolog has, however, as I have indicated above, led us into what I regard as a serious heresy— the heresy of regarding Christian orthodoxy as primarily a matter of correct thinking, rather than a matter of correct behavior. This has, I believe, even led many evangelicals to unconsciously advocate a kind of "salvation by knowledge" doctrine in place of what Scripture teaches—salvation by faithfulness.

Dialog, too, can be a primarily intellectual knowledge kind of thing. Even though the method may be superior communicationally, if the content is purely cognitive, we may still have botched the message that we are called to communicate. With life involvement, however, it is much more difficult to present a purely cognitive message, since the overall message presented

55

via this means relates so thoroughly to all of life. This method, therefore, provides a considerable corrective to the intellectualizing of the Christian message, provided our example is a properly Christian one. The contrast that I am getting at between the kinds of messages via these methods was nicely pointed out to me by an African who said, "You Euro-Americans are primarily concerned with intellectual heresy. We Africans are more concerned with interpersonal heresy." I think what he was getting at is at the heart of the Scriptural message— that the real Christian message lies in the behavior of the messenger rather than in his words. Christians who behave as Christians relate in Christian ways to other people, whether or not these people agree with them intellectually. Euro-American Christianity, however, has turned so completely to a concern for knowledge, information and doctrine, that it frequently occurs that we defend our doctrine at the expense of relating to even fellow Christians in a Christian way. It is my feeling, therefore, that even a discussion of the communicational techniques that we employ should lead us into a critical evaluation of the actual message that our receptors perceive us to be advocating.

What if One is Limited to Monolog?

Having considered all of these things with respect to the ideal way to communicate the message to which we are committed, I began to ask myself if there is anything that we can do to increase the effectiveness of our communication in situations where monolog is the only method available to us. That is, suppose I find myself in a church situation or even a classroom situation, or even worse in a situation where I must attempt to communicate via writing, can I make any adjustments that will increase the impact of my communication while minimizing the less desireable characteristics of the medium that I employ? The answer that I came to was that there is indeed much that can be done to bring our audiences to experience more of the kind of impact that characterizes dialog and life involvement communication, even when we are limited to monolog presentations. Though, for example, monolog interaction does not permit a high degree of life involvement between communicator and receptors, it is possible to increase the amount of such involvement and thereby to increase the communicational impact.

I have suggested that the above chart of approaches to communication presents us with a kind of scale with monolog at one end of the scale and life involvement at the other end. If, therefore, we look at certain of the items on that chart, we will discover that at least certain of the characteristics of dialog and life involvement can be approximated in a monolog situation. If this is done, then, at least certain of the numbers of our audiences may be able to fill in the gaps and by imagining themselves in a full life involvement situation with us to get beyond the more crippling effects of formalized monolog.

If, for example, at point 2 on the chart, the communicator refrains from presenting simply general messages and makes his messages more specific to the actual lives of his receptors, he is likely to increase the impact of his presentation. This will, of course, mean that he will need to take more time in his presentations, dealing with a smaller amount of material (see point 4) rather than the smaller amount of time dealing with larger amounts of material that often characterizes monolog presentations. He will illustrate his points more fully and, in keeping with point 6 and much of the material presented in chapters one and two concerning identification, let his receptors hear considerably more about his own personal experience than is often done in monolg.

This will, of course, involve the reduction of the formality of the situation (point 5). Even though the method of presentation is monologic, the speaker may come across more as one who is conducting a conversation, one who is participating with his hearers not only in verbalizing, but even in other areas of life. He may, as is frequently the case in conversations, reduce his material to a single point which he wraps in true to life illustrations, many of which relate to his own personal experience. I have been exposed to one preacher who did this extremely well. He never had more than one point but he illustrated it in a variety of ways and from a variety of perspectives. Because those illustrations bring about a kind of pseudo-life involvement, we found it very easy to get wrapped up in what the speaker was communicating and to get beyond such superficial characteristics of the communicational situation as the speaker's reputation and his focus on his message (point 7). I remember feeling frequently that I and I alone was in focus. I, furthermore, found myself getting much more involved (point 8) in the application of what the speaker was saying to my own experience and the integration of his perspectives into my perspective. Jesus, of course, did this very well when he used true to life stories that we call parables.

Now, we should be warned that not all decrease of formality and increase of the personalness of the communicator automatically increases the impact of communication. Often such breaking of the rules can be taken quite badly by the receptors. Say, for example, the communicator stands on the pulpit rather than standing behind it. His receptors might take this quite badly. Or, for example, suppose the communicator is not careful about the personal things that he reveals concerning himself. He might in public reveal intimate details that are considered quite inappropriate in public and thereby seriously hinder the communication. Or, suppose he is perceived to be showing off his ability to tell clever stories rather than enhancing his message by means of these stories. His communication is likely to be seriously hindered thereby or, at least, the message that is actually communicated may be something quite different from the message that he supposedly intended. If a communicator is psychologically insecure, for example, he may latch onto some of the techniques that I am recommending as means of enhancing his own prestige rather than enhancing the communication of the message.

A further adaptation that can often be made is to increase the effectiveness of the feedback and adjustment process (point 11). Some speakers are quite effective in raising questions that the audience is generally concerned with. A speaker may say, for example, something like, "You are probably asking concerning this subject such and such a question." If he has hit on a question that his audience actually is asking, they will say to themselves, "Sure enough, I am asking that question. I wonder what he is going to say about it." So the involvement of the receptor is increased (point 8) by the communicator's setting up of a fictitious though realistic feedback situation. Or, the communicator might elicit actual feedback by asking a question that the audience will answer. This technique may be less feasible in a preaching situation, particularly on Sunday morning. However, not infrequently it is possible to raise questions that the audience can answer with a nod of the head or a shake of the head rather than verbally. Often, furthermore, it is possible for a communicator to develop a sensitivity to the feedback that his hearers send via the expressions on their faces or other gestures to such an extent that he can respond by adjusting his message on the spot. Some communicators even plant people in the audience to provide such feedback for them. Pastors wives are often good at this.

In monolog situations we may also increase the possibility of discovery (point 12). Sometimes it is a good idea for us to ask questions that we don't even intend to answer directly. In this way we may stimulate people to think about these questions and to go out and grapple with them on their own. Jesus very often did this. Sometimes, furthermore, he would answer a question with another question. Even this might be possible in certain monolog presentations. Often via a series of monolog presentations it may be possible to lead people into discovery of a new perspective. Questions relating to the adequacy of the old perspective and pointed illustrations demonstrating the greater adequacy of the new perspective can play an important part in leading people to this kind of discovery.

These techniques, and probably several others that I have not mentioned, can do much to bring about the right kind of identification between the receptor and the communicator (point 13). As I have pointed out in chapters one and two, communicational impact is directly related to the ability of the receptor to identify with the source. As I have mentioned, self-exposure on the part of the communicator is often crucial to bringing about such "reverse identification." When people in the audience can say, "He may be a preacher (or teacher, etc.), but he is just like me," the potential impact of even monolog communication can be increased enormously. Or, if a significant number of those in the audience have entered into life involvement experiences with the communicator (even, for example, on the golf course), the effectiveness of material presented via monolog can be enhanced. When the communicator is known as a human being, rather than simply a reputation (point 6), even monolog communication can be very effective because it then becomes a part of a total life involvement.

In summary, it has been my intent in this and the preceding chapters to advocate incarnational, life involvement communication as the right way to go for Christian communicators. I have attempted to develop this point from the perspective of communication theory, on the one hand, and from the example of God through Christ on the other. I have generalized to a considerable extent in order to cover a large amount of material in a fairly short presentation. I have, furthermore, employed a technique that is more like those techniques that I do not recommend than it is like those that I do recommend. I have, for the sake of getting some of these ideas across to a wider audience, employed techniques that I recognized to be less effective than techniques that would involve person to person life involvement between myself and you as the receptors. Nevertheless, I am in hopes that the felt needs that exist within you will make it possible for at least some of this material to be useful to you.